THE WORK CONNECTION

Escape the modern job search

take back control

and get the work life you want

workconnectionacademy.com

simple guides to a better work life

Copyright © 2020

The Work Connection Team. The Work Connection – Escape the modern job search, take back control and get the work life you want.

All rights reserved.

No part of this publication may be reproduced, distributed, or transmitted in any form or by any means, including photocopying, recording, or other

electronic or mechanical methods, without the prior written permission of the publisher, except in the case of brief quotations embodied in critical reviews and certain other non-commercial uses permitted by copyright law.

The Work Connection Team would like to thank everyone who helped along the way especially everyone at home working on our dream. It really does take a

village, Jeff, Chris, Tiago, Andrew & Rachel who were patient and supportive all the way through the process in writing my first book. To Sarah and her family, Peter & Magda, Ben and Afsheen, Michael and Maya and Lucy and the employer contributors for their time. To anyone we have missed – thank you too.

Book Cover by Tiago. Illustrations by Andrew.

Printed in the United States of America

First Printing 2020

First Edition 2020

10 9 8 7 6 5 4 3 2 1

Disclaimer Notice:

Please note the information contained within this document is for educational and entertainment purposes only. Every attempt has been made to provide

accurate, up to date and reliable information. No warranties of any kind are expressed or implied. Readers acknowledge that the author is not engaging in the rendering of legal, financial, medical, or professional advice. The content of this book has been derived from various sources. Please consult a licensed professional before attempting any techniques outlined in this book. By reading this document, the reader agrees that under no circumstances is the author responsible for any losses, direct or indirect, which are incurred as a result of the use of information contained within this document, including, but not limited to, —errors, omissions, or inaccuracies.

THE WORK CONNECTION

Book 2 of the Work Connection series of books.
Simple guides to a better work life.

Table of Contents

Preface — 1

Chapter 1: Clarity. Part 1 — 11
The Paradox of the Hidden Job Market. It isn't as hidden as you think

Chapter 2: Clarity. Part2 — 22
Where Am I Going and Why?

Chapter 3: Attract. Part 1 — 37
How to get to your destination?

Chapter 4: Attract. Part 2 — 53
Creating More Pull

Chapter 5: Land It. Part 1 — 77
Turning Interviews into Offers

Chapter 6: Land It. Part 2 — 91
Turning Interviews into Offers

Chapter 7: Land It. Part 3 — 98
Assess, Accept, or Reject

Chapter 8: Maintain — 109

Chapter 9: The Work Connection! — 112

End Notes — 116

Preface

The Work Connection has been written for, with and by those people who want to become fulfilled and happy in their jobs, no matter what the economic conditions.

This is not an existential, 'how do I find my purpose?' book. This is a practical, real-life career design book written by industry insiders so that you too can have the work life you deserve.

The central problem *The Work Connection* sets out to address is: if you want to find a new or better job and you are not getting interviews or feedback you want, what can *you* do to get better results?

In this situation there are usually two options you can use. **Option A) or Job Search version 1.0** = 30% of all vacancies are visible to you online.

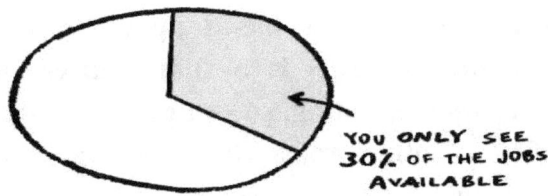

Option A is what most people do. It means keep applying for jobs online and network with people you know. Focusing your energies on that 30% in the diagram above. Option A is by its nature a mainly reactive process, you are waiting for relevant job advertisements and waiting for responses, with some small networking with people you already know.

- **Leaving the other 70% not visible to you or inaccessible in the "Hidden Job Market"**
- On average, 2% of all candidates get called to a job interview from an online job advertisement. Leaving 98% not getting an interview
- Pre-2020 pandemic, an average of 250 people applied for the same job advertised online. This will only increase during any downturn, perhaps by as much as a factor of two. Post pandemic my team and I have had jobs posted online with 400 plus applications

It is a fool's game to base your entire job hunt or career change strategy on competing with hundreds of other candidates with Job Search version 1.0. If you are searching for a job the same way everyone else is, it is time to upgrade the way you search.

The Work Connection is based upon Option B) or Job Search version 2.0. This is a simple direct to employer system of network building, so you can begin to access more of the 70% of other roles that are available. This is a proactive job hunt and career change system.

"Why do I need this? I'm busy enough doing what I am doing?" That maybe something that is going through your mind.

This is normal when presented with new ideas. There are a couple of things we have learned through researching & testing this system with job hunters and career changers over the years we would like to share.

Post Covid-19, not for the first time, we find ourselves in challenging times. Many of our economies are experiencing increased volatility and more competition for good jobs. The truth is you have little control over the economy or these events. What you can control is how prepared you are for them when they happen. What professional relationships, systems, skills, and strategies do you have in place to give yourself options should you need them?

The modern paradox is that many of us do not invest in our networks or in our interview or selling skills to anywhere near the level we invest in our education. "Why should I? If I need a job I just apply, and I'll get an interview where I want? Right? That works some of the time. In tougher economic times, what happens when it does not? Or you accept the first job that comes along, when you know there was a great company in your community you wanted to work for but just could not get in. *The Work Connection* will help you put a plan together to address that.

This is your career coach and futureproof career plan in one book.

There are two types of career change events that can happen in your work life. The first type is **Involuntary,** meaning you have limited control of the events that are happening. They can come in the form of an economic or global event like a pandemic, a recession, being made redundant or a change in your family circumstances. The other type is a **Voluntary** event, and this is where you have more control e.g. you might decide you want to upgrade your role, boss, location or take a redundancy. Whether involuntary or voluntary events happen *The Work Connection* will help you navigate your career to the destination you desire by following the four steps below.

***The Work Connection* will help you through our C.A.L.M. (Clarity, Attract, Land and Maintain) system.**

Clarity - How to review yourself and career to identify where you are going and why? How to set a plan to get there? This will reduce the feelings of anxiety and being overwhelming that modern job hunters and career changers can experience.

Also, it gives you back real FOCUS.

Attraction – How to develop better sales, marketing, and interview skills to get your foot in the door of the employer you want. Then, how to build a professional network that gives you viable options when you need them. Reducing your dependencies on technology and online job boards.

Increased levels of control.

Land - How to land the role you want through advanced interview and closing techniques. We show you how to increase your response rate from 2% in traditional job search to 8% in our system.

Maintain. A simple how to plan so you maintain your relationships and have options if you need them and help others where you can? The creation and maintenance of your professional network that gives you real options when needed.

The Work Connection comes with **two significant promises.**

First, even in the best of times, finding and landing a job that builds your career and is fulfilling, is a challenge. What follows is an insider's guide to pulling the power and control of your career back in your hands. Having a multiplying effect on your ability to get interviews and job offers. **Establishing once and for all; there is a clear difference between who I want to work for? Versus which employers are advertising for roles?**

Second, even though we leave our education systems with qualifications, degrees, and certifications, most of us have little or no understanding of how the hiring process really works. **If you follow the system presented here, you will gain a clear**

advantage over those people vying for the same opportunities and maintain a professional network that will give you more options no matter how the economy is performing.

We do not make these promises lightly. If recent events and history have shown us anything, it is to expect the unexpected in our work lives. After Covid-19, companies both big and small are going to change the way they hire and retain people. Change is inevitable, how prepared you are for it is up to you.

The Work Connection provides a system and tools that will address these new career change and job hunt challenges:

- What do I do if I am not getting interviews in my job search? Do I settle for what responses I get, or do I build my own network of opportunities directly?

- Expose the myth - Why would employers want to speak to me directly early/mid post-recession?

- How do I future-proof my career and get myself more options to help lessen the impact of events like we have witnessed in 2002, 2009, and 2020?

- What options do I have in my career? If I lost my job? What can I do to upgrade my career?

- How can I find a better employer, boss, colleagues, fulfillment, money, rewards, and location?

Why this book and why did I choose to write it?

I am a partner at one of the world's largest and most respected recruitment businesses. For the last 20 years my teams and I have recruited everyone from technology engineers to CEOs of publicly traded businesses, and most levels in between.

The idea for *The Work Connection* started with candidates communicating how frustrated they were with the modern job search. Applying for jobs that they know they can do and hearing nothing back was of huge frustration for job hunters and career changers at all levels. The increasing levels of automation, lack of feedback from employers, and the dehumanization of the process were amongst some of the main pain points. **Due to the pace of modern life and being focused on other areas, we began to see there was some consistency with these people. We noticed how little time most of them were taking to build their own professional networks. This was having an adverse effect when they needed help in their own roles or finding real job offers because they simply did not have the relationships in their network to help. They just depended on who was hiring?**

At the same time, I was seeing first-hand how some of the most successful global executives spent a small amount of time systematically every few months building relationships around them.

What if you could network like the world's best? Make it systematic. Make it simple. That way no matter what the volatility or event in the economy you would always have better relationships.

Better relationships = Better options = Better Work life.

We have worked with job hunters, career changers, leading employers and hiring managers and compiled a series of powerful insights in an easy to follow system that provides you with a clear advantage over other candidates. **Effectively learning by what has worked & what mistakes other people have made by going direct to employers.** If you follow it alongside your traditional job search you will have a backup plan, greater control, and experience far better outcomes in your job hunt.

Connecting with employers on what *they* need post Covid-19, reviewing resumes, and interviewing for real positions my team and I have insights from inside the system that we will share with you. When we share email & LinkedIn templates that get interviews or resumes and interviewing tips, we do so because they work in the real world.

Changing anything is not always straightforward, like a good coach we have set up some challenges for you along the way. These will be marked clearly in the book and will help you review key points e.g. Where are you going and why? How to improve your resume etc. They will challenge you to take a few minutes away and work on your skills. The goal is to share these simple steps & what has worked for other people and to get you closer to your work goals.

In writing *The Work Connection* we hope to help you navigate these noisy times with more options and enjoy helping others along the way. We hope you get some value from the book and more importantly start using some of the tools in the book for yourself or recommend it to a friend who needs some new ideas and support in their work life.

YOUR FREE BOOK AND TEMPLATES USED IN THIS BOOK ARE WAITING

To say thank you for taking your valuable time in reading *The Work Connection* and share some extra value, we have a free giveaway.

Visit workconnectionacademy.com/bullet to download the resume templates used in this book and our latest book in the *The Work Connection* Academy series – From Zero to Interview; *The proven three-step guide to getting the interviews you want, now.*

This book is packed with real life case studies, resume and email templates to help you get interviews when you are not getting responses to your applications. **If you have any questions raised by the book, pop over to workconnectionacademy.com/bullet and we will respond ASAP.**

Let's   get   **started!**

Chapter 1: Clarity. Part 1

The Paradox of the Hidden Job Market. It isn't as hidden as you think

Aside from the 2020 pandemic and its resulting economic crisis, there are some demographic and generational changes happening that are relevant to anyone searching for a new job.

When applying to online job advertisements you should not expect a communication flow. In the last few years, many employers and HR departments have been scaled back to unprecedented levels. After the 2009 and 2020 recessions, like most other departments, HR professionals have been loaded with additional responsibilities and their work-life became tougher than ever. Leaving the average HR and Talent Acquisition person overloaded and under-resourced.

Many such managers find it difficult to get their own work done, never mind responding to the high volume of job applicants.

Our education systems. The feedback we get from people leaving our education systems is mixed in terms of how well the system equips leavers with the adequate skills needed to build a professional network and land the job they want. Many of these education systems have a focus on getting the academic part of education executed. This in turn leaves less time, resource, and expertise for the practical. How do you now take this knowledge into the real world and build a career/ targeted network?

Many schools, colleges and universities vary from leaving it to the student to reach out and create their own relationships through to the more hands-on counselor and alumni groups, who have embedded relationships with employers. The latter offers more traditional services like employability classes, resume writing, and employer fairs where employers can come, creating an initial opportunity to connect and build knowledge. Many people in the first group are left to themselves to acquire the knowledge on the *who* and *how* to build their careers and networks as they move along.

People are moving jobs now more than at any other time in human history. According to an article in *Forbes*.com, "more than 40% of baby boomers have stayed with an employer for more than twenty years."[i] In comparison, a recent Fortune article notes that, "millennials will expect to stay in jobs for less than three years." [ii] In other words, millennials (generally considered to be those born between 1984 and 2004) and younger generations will expect to change jobs fifteen to twenty times in their lives.

The competition for roles is increasing in major markets. In most countries, economic immigration is growing. In the North American market, Stats Canada indicates that "more than 235,000 people came into Canada per year in the years 2014 – 2016." [iii] Migrationpolicy.org states that, "on average, 1.3 million people entered the U.S. in the years 2015 – 2016."[iv]. The competition for advertised roles is getting fiercer every year.

Technology's impact on the hiring process and modern work, like everything, has its positives and flaws. As Mark Andreessen, founder at Netscape and renowned venture capitalist, wrote, "Software is eating the world, in all sectors. Technology has evolved to such a rate that whole companies base their talent strategies around it, rather than around the talent!"[v]

Hiring is still a largely manual process, but the sorting, prioritizing, and selection of talent is relying more and more on software and artificial intelligence (things like keyword tracking and A.T.S. Applicant Tracking Systems).

From our experience, good hiring managers, recruiters and employers need good people. Technology may have given employers access to information and to automate the process, but in many cases, it has not helped them get the right people to the right seats. Even with the technology in place, there are still skills shortages in many areas.

With the human element being removed from so many of our communications and systems, the people who apply for roles are left repeatedly frustrated at the application process. Cover letters and resumes often must be retyped into automated systems, even when the details are available on their resume. It is not possible for the employer, hiring manager or head-hunter to respond to everyone. That would be a full-time job on its own for each role posted. In developing the C.A.L.M. system we have built this as a core function of our system. Building relationships and direct contact with target employers for the long term, so you have a backup plan.

The Hidden Job Market - What is the 70% made up of?

There are two main ways to access the other hidden job market or other 70% of roles, from the outside of a target employer. First is to be referred to the employer by someone you know. This means that it is important to build your network in a methodical manner. If you stick with the family, school, work colleagues or friends you have when you are 25, it will be difficult for you to develop a full professional network as you progress through your career.

The second way is to introduce yourself to a targeted hiring manager group that you did not previously know. We will go into these methods in more detail later in this chapter with a case study.

It is also quite normal to wonder why and how you would start a conversation with an alternative employer when you have a job. The why is based around options. Post Covid-19, we know volatility is growing and you either have options or you do not. Hiring manager's love, it when relevant well researched candidates approach them directly.

The C.A.L.M system (Clarity, Attract, Land and Maintain) will give you clear steps so you can move outside your comfort zone, one step at a time.

This mindset change from viewing networking as only necessary when you need a job, to a habit you do repeatedly will have a marked effect in decreasing your anxiety and stress level, improving your career trajectory and work enjoyment.

Our first case study is Peter, a recent graduate of *The Work Connection*. Peter used our system from start to finish and is a great example of adapting to the changes mentioned above.

"Leaving Poland in 1985 was not as easy as it is today," Peter said. Back in the mid '80s, Peter was a young engineer in a closed and difficult communist state, a place bedeviled by inflation, food stamps, and queues. He and his wife, Magda, had been married for just over a year when they decided to emigrate to find opportunity and some semblance of security elsewhere.

Peter and Magda arrived in Toronto in 1985. In the following three decades, he and Magda raised three children, and he worked his way up in an engineering and manufacturing firm to an operations manager position. But when the owner of his company died unexpectedly and the company went into liquidation, Peter was laid off after 32 years. Now, seven months into his job search, he was growing increasingly frustrated. He was a qualified mechanical engineer, with great expertise, but the stress for him and his family was intense.

This was the first time Peter had ever been out of work. The primary revenue earner for his house and over 50-years old, he had little in the way of pension savings and figured that employers might not consider him because of his age. Peter had many transferable skills and being an engineer, he approached his job search as a problem to be solved. There was certainly no lack of motivation. What he lacked though, was a system.

As the months went by, Peter only grew more anxious. Employers were not responding to his online applications and interviews were hard to come by. Dredging through Indeed.com and LinkedIn.com, finding the same jobs every day, took its toll. "Why were companies not replying?" Peter thought. He had experience and the right qualifications. So why the radio silence?

Peter needed to change his behavior to get a different result. The reason why people like Peter lack a real return in their search is two-fold. First, their job-hunting skills are not what they should be; and second, they have been busy working and not building a targeted professional network. When needed, they have little or no relationships developed outside of their current employers.

The first stage of the *The Work Connection* process was bringing Peter up to speed on the modern hiring system that he was entering and the 70/30 law. When he began to see that he was spending too much of his time in 30% of the entire job market, we started to look at strategies to get him access to the other 70% of roles.

Step 1. The Who

In weeks one and two Peter started with what sectors he would like to work in and where he would have the greatest transferability of skills. He had worked in industrial manufacturing all his life, so that was one. He also had an interest in cars from a young age, so he added automotive manufacturing. Finally, there was a large collection of food and beverage manufacturing businesses near his home. He would be able to work in operations or engineering in any of those industries. This immediately widened his opportunity list whilst maintaining his interest levels and his ability to earn.

We tasked him with finding thirty-five companies that he would like to work with, in each sector. Using Google, LinkedIn, and Glassdoor for two weeks he built out his Target List. Each employer had one target contact.

As Peter was aiming for an Operations Manager role, he needed to target contacts of people he would report into, e.g. Operations Director, VP Operations etc. These people are known as Hiring Managers.

Going from no options Peter now had built one hundred and five potential employers to consider.

Step 2. The How

In weeks three and four Peter began approaching the employers directly. At first, Peter's confidence was a little low and he felt hesitant, he didn't know whether these employers even wanted to hear from him. Nevertheless, he started with an email introduction and a follow up LinkedIn message, and then a phone call. By week four, his first responses were polite 'no, thanks' or 'we'll keep your details on file' type communications. Then at the end of week four he got his first meeting/interview requests.

Step 3. The Outcome.

That was the first of four interview requests in the next three weeks. As he interviewed, he began to build up his knowledge and build relationships with employers he had driven past every day for more than three decades. Two of the meetings turned into job offers and he accepted one. The company where he accepted the offer was going through a change of ownership and needed someone who is technically strong in engineering to help build out their product base for an expansion into the U.S. market. The job is just 8 km from his house, he is earning $10k more in salary than before (plus a pension plan) and he loves the people he is working with.

I caught up with him recently, he has been with the employer just over two years, has been promoted and is helping them build a new manufacturing plant. **"What I learned through the process is that I should have been building my connections from the beginning of my career. A small amount every year"** Peter said. **"Then, if needed, I would have had people to reach out to. Even now that I am happy in my work and have just been promoted, every three months I connect with a minimum of three local employers to check in and see what they are doing. By year end I know I have twelve relationships made each year. I plan on working for a while yet and it gives Magda and I some real peace of mind."**

Peter had the view previously that he had "no need to network and build relationships outside of work" with other people for over 30 years. Like most people he was happy in his job and was busy doing that and raising a family.

He realized he had worked hard in getting his engineering degree and in his job, but he had neglected building relationships with people in his sector. When involuntary events happen like his boss dying, a pandemic or a recession, he would have had a group of relationships who could potentially hire him or know of people who could hire him.

This is a constant cultivation process. One where you get to choose who you network with. You have the power to set criteria and see who gets into or is removed from your network. If you are a qualified Pharmaceutical Engineer and want to work in that field in Manchester, U.K. or Sydney, Australia you can build your own network of Pharmaceutical businesses and Engineering Managers within those companies and areas, no one is stopping you. If you add one person per workweek in the average working year, that equals 40 plus hiring managers per year.

Takeaways:

- **Key Principle: Reactive to Proactive.** Make the decision that you will take back control of your career change or job hunt

- **Start by building an understanding of how the hiring system works.** The hiring system is like any other system; it has its positives and its areas of improvement. Study it so you know where you can make the best of it

- **How recession-proof are you?** Be honest, if you lost your job, or if you could lose your job - do you have strong relationships with people who would hire you in good employers at the right hiring level? Or not? If not, do not worry, we will show you how to build them

- **Remember to be C.A.L.M. (Clarity, Attract, Land and Maintain)** Nurture your relationships and your career will prosper. Building a targeted network is a career long process. It is not an overnight process, so be C.A.L.M.

*Pro Tip if you already know what work you want to do and why? Skip to Chapter 3. On page 36.

Chapter 2: Clarity. Part2

Where Am I Going and Why?

If you have a destination or a vision for what you want from your work life, you can handle any deviations that might come your way. On the other hand, if you have no destination in mind, be prepared for other factors like the economy, a pandemic, an unsecure employer, or the job market to set your destination for you.

Setting your Destination

When going through a change in your work life, a career change, voluntary or involuntary event, things can get overwhelming. This chapter will provide some tools and tactics to help with control of this overwhelming feeling and to better understand where you are going.

It is always best to start with where you have come from, in career terms. This evaluation process, coupled with a more in-depth look at yourself, will start to build a strong foundation to guide your search.

To help guide you through this, we have created a simple four-stage process called The Career Compass.

The Career Compass

The Skills Audit: Building a better understanding of yourself, your skills, and talents, and how you get enjoyment from work.

The Career Map: This is a look back at your decision making in securing, your performance in, and why you left your previous roles. Looking at what influenced your decision-making at the time. And are there any patterns you can learn from?

Reasons for looking: Why are you looking at new opportunities? Your top three priorities and what is not so important in your job hunt or career change.

The Goal: Setting your Destination Statement – where you are going and why you are going there?

Try to challenge yourself to be honest and view your career with a fresh perspective. Taking a step back and being objective helps to make better decisions and will help you to avoid any biases that your brain has placed on the events of the past; giving you the ability to understand what *actually* happened versus what you *perceived* happened.

The Career Compass

Step 1. The Skills Audit

The first tool we use in the Career Compass is **The Skills Audit.** This is a simple tool designed to help you reflect on your own skills and traits. *We encourage you to take notes in this section.

Before you start your search, take some time to reflect on who you are and how a job can maximize your value and joy.

- What are your three greatest talents and traits?
- How can you maximize these traits?
- What work examples best describe your personality?
- What has been the work where you experienced the greatest enjoyment?
- What location did you most enjoy? Office, team or working from home?
- Which jobs match with the answers to above questions?

If you are looking for inspiration, think back to the teams or projects you have been engaged with. This will give you a starting point to see the value, talents, and personality you bring to a job.

This is the beginning of building a solid understanding of who you are in a work context. It will provide a foundation to support your ultimate job search. In our experience, it will help you limit your capacity to make reactive decisions based on the job market, available job postings, and factors outside your control. It will move you towards designing the career that will deliver for you.

Step 2. The Career Map

The second tool we use in the Career Audit is **The Career Map.** This is a tool designed to help you reflect on where you have come from before determining where you are going.

Draw a continuous line from left to right on a page, adding each job as an offshoot to the line, including the reason(s) you accepted, your effectiveness in the job, and the reason why you left the job.

Be honest, if the real reason for accepting a job was "it was the only offer I had and I needed a job," write that down. If you left a job because you didn't like your boss or you lacked the interest or the grit to see it through, note that, too.

Also, make a note if there was anything else that had an impact on your decision-making at the time. One example might be that you wanted a new challenge, or you didn't like the work, or the commute was too long, or you weren't paid enough.

You are looking for the truths and reasons influencing your decision-making. Take the time and focus on the main influences that made you accept or leave each job.

Now review your career map while answering the following questions:

- What does your map reveal about your decisions and your approach to your career?

- Are there any patterns to your behaviors or decision-making? For example, a lack of job offers leading to accepting what you get, instead of what you want. Or leaving your job because of redundancy or the relationship with your boss.

- What motivations have you given the greatest priority in your career progression? Some examples might be how much money you made, what you learned in the position, what the relationship with your boss and colleagues was like, what you found out about the culture of the business, whether or not the commute was doable, whether or not the job gave you a sense of worth, or upward mobility.

Then, it's good to decide and make note of which three, in ranked order, you want to guide your decision-making in your career. Make a note of these, we will refer to them later in the process.

_____

_____

_____

_____

_____

Step 3. Reasons for Looking

The "Reasons for Looking" for a new job are building blocks in making better decisions.

The key to the effectiveness of this is to get deeper insights into yourself; answers like "because I'm out of work" will only get you so far. Go deeper. Look at the following Reasons for Looking example questions and answers, and notice how we drill down to get to the core of what a new job might look like.

Focus Question: What one thing in your work life if corrected would make the most impact on your career enjoyment?

A better paid job in project management in the technology sector.

Other examples of questions to consider when building your Destination Statement.

Work: What have I learned from my current or last role in the type of work I would like to do?

I would like to do more work in project management in software applications development.

Boss: What type of boss did I produce my best work with?

I would like to work for a boss who gives me more autonomy.

Culture: What work culture best suits me?

I would like to work for a business that rewards individual initiative.

Package: How much do I need to be paid now? How much do I need to be paid in five years' time? Does this target role give me control of that five-year target?

I would like to work for a package of $120k+.

Location: What location is optimal, and would I move for the right role?

I would like to work for a company within 30 minutes of travel from home.

Development: What progression/development is important for me?

I would like to work for a company that invests in the training and development of its people.

Flexibility: How do I want to work? From an office or home or hybrid?

I would like to have flexibility to work from home when needed.

Sustainability: Does this company have the health of the environment, for example, as one of its core values?

I would like to work for an ethical employer.

Challenge #1: Create Your Own Destination Statement Step 4: Set your Destination Statement.

Get some paper and a pen and from the nine Reasons for Looking, list in the last two pages, prioritize your top three reasons below.

The focus question should be number 1, then follow with two others that are important to you. Once you have ranked the top three reasons that are important to you, this prioritized list is your **Destination Statement**.

Be ruthless and honest. By prioritizing those things which are of greatest importance to you and your family, you will be able to develop a very clear picture of what success looks like in your work and home life. Learning to say no to some other reasons above will allow you to say yes to the areas you really want. Once you've ranked the top three priorities that are important to you, insert your own Destination Statement below.

_____

_____

This second case study is with Ben and his wife, Afsheen. This case study shows how the Career Compass was successfully used to guide and set the destination for one of our theworkconnectionacademy.com graduates.

Ben is a highly trained and experienced product development engineer, but when we connected, he seemed anxious and stressed. He and his wife, Afsheen, were based just outside

London, U.K. When we first connected, they were expecting their second child and were starting to wonder how they could afford their expanding family on his current salary. Ben also worked a long way from home and his commute was grueling. There was no way to get home quickly if he had to, and the flexibility of working from home was not an option with his current employer.

Then their situation got worse, Ben was made redundant in the second month of his wife's pregnancy.

Ben had to begin searching for a new job and we helped him set about evaluating his Skills Audit, Career Map, and then his Reasons for Looking. Since this was a family decision, Ben and Afsheen discussed the questions together and identified the Reasons for Looking priorities. Again, the initial thinking was 'Ben needs a job yesterday that is the reason for looking!' Stepping back and really looking at what an ideal job search would look like helped give them both some focus and peace of mind.

Ben then prioritized the list and used it to point him in the right direction of which employers to target.

Ben and Afsheen's list:

Package: Ben earned £48k a year with his old role and had a second child on the way, and a mortgage. He needed a minimum range of £55k– £60k to cover the added expenses of a child and allow them to maintain their existing lifestyle.

Location: Ben's old job location required a long commute. A new role with options for flexible hours or working from home would be ideal.

Management: Ben was looking for a supportive and flexible boss.

Team and People: As a positive person, Ben would like to work with good people in a supportive, team-based environment.

Work: Ben is highly skilled and loved the day to day work of design and development. He would like to find that same kind of work in the new position.

Culture, Development, and Progression: Being made redundant due to a Covid-19, Ben wanted to work for an employer that was more secure.

Following the Career Compass model, Ben and Afsheen had a new perspective on his Reasons for Looking and could now turn those reasons into opportunities. By prioritizing his Reasons for Looking, they now had a targeted career destination that became a Destination Statement.

Salary: For both Ben and Afsheen, the most critical factor impacting their home and Ben's career was related to their finances. Ben needed a job that paid more than $55K.

Location: With no family nearby, Afsheen is often left alone to care for the family. It is critical for Ben to be within a thirty-minute drive from home.

Flexibility: As a highly skilled and experienced engineer, Ben is very independent. He is looking for a job that offers him the opportunity to work from home when possible.

Ben's destination statement.

I would like a product development engineering job, **within 30 mins of home, paying between £55k to £65k base. Ideally with a company that has a flexible work from policy.**

Step 1. The Who

Ben now had a clear sense of his destination: He wanted a better paid, more flexible product engineering role with a consumer business, and he wanted to be closer to home. Now he needed to build relationships with the employers who met his needs.

Like Peter, Ben identified two or three sectors in which he would like to work. Ben had worked in consumer-packaged goods for most of his working life. When he looked online at employers in that sector who were close to where he lived, he could see that there were enough nearby to approach, but he also realized that he needed a secondary sector to build out his chances of getting a better paying role. Ben also had transferable skills in manufacturing, where he could use his product design skills to work autonomously from home.

Like Peter he spent weeks 1 and 2 using the same online services and found 35 employers that he would like to work with in each of his target sectors. Then in each company, he added 1 target contact who were Product Development Managers or Head of Product Engineering in the bigger employers. 35 employers x 2 sectors = 70 employers, which gave him 70 contacts. As he added the contacts' name's he added their contact details, LinkedIn, email and phone.

Step 2. The How

For weeks 2-4, he began approaching his list. First step was an email introduction, a followed-up LinkedIn approach, and then a phone call.

By weeks 4 and 5, he was receiving his first responses. They were all no, or radio silence but he was expecting that. He had worked in Manufacturing and Consumer Packaged Goods employers before and knew that people spend time on the shopfloor or with clients and not in their inboxes, so he stayed patient. Then at the end of week 6 he had his first two meeting requests back to back. One was for a consumer-packaged goods employer close to home. Ben also really liked their product range and brand.

Step 3. The Outcome.

Ben and the employer had a great interview process, meeting a hiring manager and leadership of a team that needed help and they offered him a role he wanted with the ability to work from home and starting at £57.5k base plus bonuses. When we caught up with Ben and Afsheen they were looking forward to the rest of the pregnancy and he commented, **"Post redundancy, I was putting a lot of pressure on myself because the bills were stacking up and I wasn't getting the interviews I needed from applying online. After setting the Destination Statement, I felt focused on what I wanted. At the start I was thinking, how am I going to find 20**

employers never mind 75? I stuck at it and in the first couple of weeks and by days 10-14 my list started to look strong. Building out my network contact list in Consumer-Packaged Goods and Manufacturing gave me confidence that I could get a better paid role as there were more employers locally than I first anticipated. The biggest takeaway for me was it was a numbers and focus system. It got to week six before I got positive responses. My local network is made up of more than 40 live contacts now. **To get a job that allows me to work flexibly and is closer to home means I get more time to support Afsheen and see more of our family. Given everything that has happened during Covid-19, for us, that is priceless."**

Challenge #2: The Clarity Tool

Read your destination statement then shut your eyes. Imagine it is one year from now and you have had the *perfect* work year in that role. Answer the following questions:

- What does your perfect work year look like?
- What are your one-year goals that would make that perfect year happen?
- Why are these goals important to you?
- What resources or skills do you need to get to your destination statement?

This detail is key; I would ask you to do this exercise before you move on.

This tool has had a huge impact in my own life. In my 20's I didn't lack motivation, I lacked a system. Before using this technique, my productivity was up and down, now I use it at the start of the year and review at the end of each quarter to see how I am progressing. It can be helpful too in years like 2020 when a global pandemic event happened in March. It helped me to recalibrate as so many changes were happening at once and it was hard to be focused on anything else than just keeping my job and helping our customers and candidates.

Takeaways:

- **Key Principle: Prioritize your goals into your Destination Statement.** If you have a destination for your work life, you can manage deviations. No destination? Be prepared for other people to set your destination for you

- **To know where you are going, you must know where you came from.** Reflect on your career, skill set, and personality. This will allow you to understand where you want your target sectors and roles to be

- **Real clarity and focus are a habit and skill that can be worked upon and improved**

- **Learning to say no will allow you to say yes to what you really want.**

- **Reduce feeling overwhelmed and increase focus and performance by using The Clarity Tool** to create an ideal year in your work life. Review and maintain this and it will have a multiplying effect on your progression

Chapter 3: Attract. Part 1

How to get to your destination?

Getting to your career destination and designing the career you want is a lot like a pilot preparing before taking off. The pilot has a destination and a flight plan to get there. Along the way, they may have minor and sometimes major deviations on the route. Along the journey, alterations must be made, yet ultimately the destination is the goal. **The bigger the changes, the better the plan needs to be.**

At this stage in your job search, you have built a Destination Statement, now it is time to look at how you are going to go about finding and identifying the employers that match your destination statement. These will be your target networks.

Start by setting up a Google Sheets or Microsoft Excel file to compile and manage the list.

Your list should include the following:

Company Name: a company that matches your destination goals – better role, better development or less stress, etc.

Location: the preferred location(s)

Sector: the sector where your target role is based

Job Title: your target job role

Hiring manager: defined as a person that your target role reports to and has the ability and budget to hire you.

Document their name, title, and contact information

In theory, you can have as many names as you want on your destination list, but a good number to go for on each list is 35 companies per sector. Ideally you should be going for 2 or 3 sector lists of 35 companies in each.

Example: Ben from Chapter 2 had lists: Consumer Packaged Goods & Manufacturing. And these lists had 70 employers and 70 contacts in total. Now you may live in a smaller community than London. The key is to make it relevant to your destination statement and your environment.

*Pro Tip as a minimum, for this to work you will need as close to 70 confirmed hiring managers. Starting with 25 people is better than none, but you need quality and volume in weeks 1 and 2 to get real momentum.

One of the things to consider when adding employers to your list - is the size of the company, or how many people they employ.

In smaller to medium companies (defined as having 250 people or less) there may be fewer gatekeepers, a receptionist who answers the phone, an executive assistant or less bureaucracy, and more access to your target group of hiring managers. **This gives you the ability to speak directly to the person you would likely be reporting into.**

Depending on your Destination Statement goals, and if targeted correctly, smaller businesses may be secure, going through change or even growing. Growing teams and businesses need good people and leaders. In addition, within smaller businesses, decision-making tends to be done from the top levels, making the organizational structure flatter, thereby giving you direct access to people truly responsible for hiring.

Medium to larger employers, in some cases, may have more gatekeepers and bureaucracy in decision making but, in turn, they usually have more defined roles, security, and structure. If in your Career Compass, you have been made redundant from two smaller Startup businesses in a short space of time, included in your Destination Statement could be finding a more secure business.

Having a mixture of both size of employer is good for variety. From a pure getting in contact viewpoint, having some more SME's on your list will increase your chances of getting connected and building relationships. In the end, it is all guided by your destination statement goals.

Who do you want on your lists? And as important, who do you not want on your lists?

A Destination Employer: This is an organization that answers your Destination Statement. There is one important group of people in a Destination Employer who you will want to include on your target list.

Contact 1: Hiring manager: A person or persons who your destination role reports to. A hiring manager must have the authority and budget to hire your level of role. Think back to Peter, he was an Operations Manager - his hiring managers were Operations Directors or V.P. Operations. For your target role who would you report into?

There is huge importance in connecting directly with hiring managers. Hiring managers have the potential to have the greatest impact on your career and destination because in employers, these people have direct responsibility for their team's success, and therefore will do their best to find, attract, and hire great people for their teams.

If for whatever reason you can't get in contact with the hiring manager at a chosen employer, then as a backup contact Head of Talent Acquisition or Head of H.R.

There are quite a few tools available on the internet to get the information you need and help you to answer these questions. Let's go through key tools, so you can set your process in place and identify how they can assist you in building your list.

Google searches will help you find an initial profile of the company including the number of employees, new product lines, expansions, headcount adding, where they rank in their sector, and even the names of the hiring managers. Alternatively, you may find articles about investment in their employees' development, culture, and product lines. Or flag events, like lawsuits, redundancies, or employee issues.

Always start with Google then move to LinkedIn. Google will be able to cast the net wider for specific searches whereas LinkedIn is a community network.

LinkedIn is an excellent resource to not only obtain information about a target company but more importantly, to identify people and possibly hiring managers employed by the company. Using LinkedIn, you can search for company profiles, hiring manager job titles, content posted by companies, and possible connections within the company who you may be able to assist. 1. Search the main search area, type the company name 2. You can adapt your location as needed.

Employer websites are another good source of information. Depending on the size of the company, you may find contact names including hiring managers' names and sometimes email addresses and telephone numbers. This is usually located in the About Us or Team part of the website. The site can also be an indicator about the company culture.

Getting contact details. To get the email contact details of a hiring manager, here is what to do:

1. When you have the names of the hiring manager or contact you would like to connect with, our readers have found vocus.io or hunter.io useful. These services get constantly updated so you can search email finders and a list will pop up. 2. Enter the company name and hit search. The site will search their database and if it is there, they will supply the email address for example, name.name@aaa.com.

This will give you email suggestions for you to add to your employer list. Remember, be patient. This is a trial and error process you will refine as you send information and check if you have the right details.

Glassdoor allows current and former employees to anonymously review companies. The insights and patterns of feedback from employees can help to create a picture of what the "state of play" is at a destination employer. (As with all online review sites, the information found should be read warily as reviewers can often have an axe to grind).

While you are searching for destination employers and hiring managers, it is worth considering another group of people who can assist you in your search, peers. **These are people who currently work in your target teams and destination employers**. They are a great source of information to help build an understanding of your potential employer, its culture, and values.

Most importantly, they can facilitate connections and meetings. Connecting with someone who currently works in your destination company helps to build strong work relationships (if you are hired) and make the best career decisions based on all the available information.

What is Value-Based Networking?

We are now ready to move from the "who and where would you like to work?" to the "how are you going to get there?" part of the system.

In his book, *Give and Take*, Adam Grant, a Wharton Business School professor, examines the remarkable forces that can shape a person's career and why some people rise to the top and others don't. Grant writes that when it comes to business relationships and behaviors, people operate as either takers, matchers, or givers.

Takers seize what they can get; matchers try to create an even exchange; givers are the outliers in that they commit themselves to giving to others unconditionally. According to Grant's research, many givers experience success no matter the industry or business. They are also amongst the very top performers in their chosen fields.

When it comes to building the professional network and career you want, this concept of giving, taking, and matching is relevant. When speaking about networking professionally, which group would you identify with? Giver, taker, or matcher? Your work life is such a big part of your life. Is it all about the money and progression? Isn't it important to leave a legacy of people you helped along the way? If we all did a little of this, everyone would benefit.

In the second part of this chapter, we'll examine what a Value-Based Network is, the philosophy behind it, and how cultivating your own **Value-Based Network is the antidote to the pains of the modern job search and taker mentality.**

A core part of the C.A.L.M. system (Clarity, Attract, Land and Maintain) to job hunting or career change is the **Value Based Network. This is defined as a group of people in your work life that you can help and who can help you.** Unfortunately, some people look at networking as something transactional and have a "taking" view of it. This has led to traditional networking been viewed negatively over the last 50 years. But the best networking is not about taking, it is about *giving value*.

TO BUILD A VALUE BASED NETWORK

TAKER
TRADITIONAL NETWORKING

- LOTS OF BUSINESS CARDS
- ELEVATOR PITCHES
- FORCED UNCOMFORTABLE ENVIRONMENT
- ANXIETY - AM I GOING TO GET ANYTHING FROM THIS GROUP?

GIVER/MATCHER
VALUE BASED NETWORKING

- YOU PICK WHO YOU WANT TO HELP AND WHO TO ASK FOR HELP
- SEEK TO UNDERSTAND BEFORE BEING UNDERSTOOD
- GENUINE INTEREST CULTIVATES NETWORK CAPITAL
- GIVING BACK IS GOOD FOR THE SOUL - PASSING IT FORWARD HELPS BUILD THE FOUNDATIONS OF YOUR NETWORK

Challenge #3: Lend a Hand

Can you think of someone in your professional network you can help this week? Reach out to them in the next 24 hours. Give yourself extra points for someone who can't help you back. This is a great start.

How did you feel after it? Can you replicate this once a month?

Helping people has an exponential effect:

- When you need help in the future, you will have enough equity in your Value Based Network to ask and get something back of value

- Giving and helping is much more fulfilling than sitting idle

- When economic times shift, the equity, and relationships you have stored and built in the group will allow you to have options

- Engaging and investing in relationships in your sector helps you build knowledge, and your value will increase as a result

How Do We Give Value?

While networking value can be assigned in several ways, here are three of the best:

Clarity: Be genuine in your interest. In truly listening and asking questions, you can figure out quickly if there is anything you can do to help.

Listening: Be prepared to ask yourself, "Can I help this person?" "What can I help them with," and "Can this person help me?"

Next Steps: Whether you can or can't help, be honest! If you can't or don't want to, don't! Your network is your network. It must be smartly and equitably managed.

Everyone started somewhere. By the way it is completely normal to wonder, "Why would I be approaching this person? What have I got to give to them?" **Be humble, approach them with something that is of value, possibly some experience in their product areas or sector, a commonality or knowing someone in common and remember that that person started somewhere just like you and that several people helped them along the way.**

Cultivation Rules

Using the Farmer's Harvest analogy, building a Value-Based Network is like cultivating your harvest from your field. Each sector you have is a field; how many seeds have you set in the last week, month or year? It is not likely that you will see your harvest overnight. However, by having consistent action and building connections with people or setting your seeds, these will in time produce your harvest. For us relationships are the harvest.

The three Ps, Patience, Persistence, and Protection are the foundation principles of any Value-Based Network. Below we will look at a case study on building your network, along with background on why these principles are crucial in cultivating your Value-Based Network.

Case Study Three. An example of building a Value Based Network from scratch, Michael, and his wife Maya. At the time of us first connecting, they lived in Cape Town, South Africa. Maya had secured a scholarship at a University in Austin, Texas. They had visited family there and loved what the city and Texas had to offer. Michael is a Chief Information Officer in the technology sector, he helps technology businesses build products and systems.

When Michael first read this book in January, he had been applying for a few roles locally in Austin but had not been able to secure any interviews as he lacked U.S. experience. This was frustrating for a person who had been very successful in his corporate career in technology.

Michael was still based in SA while starting his job hunt in the U.S. He went through the same steps as Peter and Ben. After completing his Career Compass and his Destination Statement, he had a focus on building a Value Based Network in the high growth Technology and Ecommerce markets in Austin. In the months between January and April, he set specific goals around how many Microsoft Teams /Zoom he could have with hiring managers in his chosen two sectors.

The key was instead of focusing on approaching people and asking strangers for jobs and getting rejected, he focused on creating a connection and a real relationship with the hiring manager through shared work. He looked at his resume and experience and there was an abundance of high growth Ecommerce and Technology experience. Austin has a thriving technology sector, think employers like EBay, Facebook, 3M, Dell and a growing consumer technology and start-up scene in all areas where Michael could connect with people with real commonality and shared experience.

Michael's big goal was to have video calls with at least three potential employers every month in that year, so that by December, when he reviewed his work year, he would have circa 36 hiring manager relationships in Austin. His micro goal was that out of those 36 calls, he would hope to get one job offer per every six calls, or one every two months.

Each day, he would use Google, LinkedIn, Employers' websites, and Glassdoor in setting the seeds and making the connections.

Michael relished this approach, committing 30 mins every workday. He could better control the outcome and used his frustration at not getting interviews as fuel to keep pushing him forward. Also, he was in his element learning about the Technology market in Austin and its nuances. To cover his bases, he still applied for roles he saw online. In fact, he used the C.A.L.M. (Clarity, Attract, Land and Maintain) system to network with the employers that were advertising as a backup.

As part of his approach, he used the following template to get the attention of the group.

Subject line: Connecting

Hi _____,

My name is Michael X. I have been interested in your company's work on the _____ technology launch. My family and I are moving to Austin as my wife has secured a scholarship at _____. I have built & launched similar technology brands, on _____ platform in the technology/ ecommerce/ retail sector. My specialism is managing technology teams through change.

The reason for contacting you is I would love to connect with you and learn more about your vision for your team and the product. I am currently interviewing for leadership roles in the Austin area.

Would the week of the 23rd or 30th work for a 15-minute conversation over Zoom, face/face or Microsoft Teams?

Thank you for taking the time to connect.

Regards,

Michael.

The outcome. Michael hit his call targets in January to March of three calls with potential employers a month. **He and his family had arrived in April as planned, and by the end of**

June, he had two offers of employment. **He accepted a permanent role on the consulting side of technology which gave him more flexibility to work and get to know the market.** Michael continues to build his relationships every quarter as he plans to stay in Austin.

There are some interesting lessons from his efforts.

From frustration to giving: Over the first 6 months, Michael had calls with well over 20 people in his sector. Interestingly, one of those calls was with an analyst from a LinkedIn mail. That analyst knew a firm that was looking for a new leader for one of their business units. Alternatively, one of the employers Michael had a call with had nothing at his level, but they did have an analyst role.

Michael did the introduction and the hiring manager hired the analyst. The analyst did the introduction to the employer of the role Michael accepted! **In less than 6 months he had gone from not getting interviews to helping another person getting a role and himself getting a role in another country.**

Focus on relationships, specifically building a connection instead of just getting interviews. By refocusing, Michael was able to improve his return when building a targeted network from another country. The interviews were a by-product of the relationships he was developing.

Industry networks are like villages: Treating everyone from the janitor to the CEO respectfully will pay off. Michael shifting his mentality to a more giving state of mind that ultimately led to the job offer he accepted.

You can start anytime! The earlier you begin building your relationships in your Value Based Network, the better. With the right connections and the right mentality, you can proactively create the career path you want rather than reactively waiting for a dream job advertisement to appear.

Takeaways:

- **Key Principle:** Value-Based Networking is the map of how you get from where you are to your destination statement

- Taking the first step in "giving" cultivates your credibility and reputation in your network

- Don't just take from your network. Contribute to it

- Ask yourself - How can I create win/win scenarios to build connections?

- "Rome was not built in a day". It is about consistency of action every month. Think little and often. The more quality relationships you have, the more options you will have now and, in the future,

- If you only look at value through the lens of what you are receiving, you are going to be unhappy

Next, we will look at how to best approach these new relationships and people using insider tools and techniques.

Chapter 4: Attract. Part 2

Creating More Pull

Time is one of the most valuable commodities there is. Post Covid-19 to get time (either Zoom/Teams meetings or interviews) with your hiring managers, it is not enough just to build great lists. You must do two things; take precise action and create a need in the other person to meet and spend some time with you.

To get this valuable time let us apply a standard marketing strategy "push & pull" to help us connect with the hiring manager group. *Push* marketing means that you are trying to promote a specific product (in this scenario, *you* are the product) to an audience (in this case, hiring managers). *Pull* marketing implies that you implement a strategy that draws consumers to your products (you), thereby often creating loyal customers or relationships. As a result, improving your chances of getting your foot in the door.

When pushing information to the hiring manager through email invites, LinkedIn messages, resumes, etc., it is good to first seek to understand what will be attractive to them, then seek to be understood. In theory, your goal is to create more of a pull. This will increase your chance of getting time with them. Think Michael from the previous chapter and his research on what the target technology employers in Austin would *really* be interested in.

We will employ three tactics to increase the pull part of this strategy.

Be proactive and do your research on your target network: Make the first steps in understanding the employers and hiring managers and their needs.

Re-work your communications including LinkedIn profiles and resumes to be more achievement orientated. You have a small window to make an impression. Let us make one where they are wanting to connect with you.

Elevate how you approach the hiring managers: using the research and our templates to get your foot in the door.

How do you first seek to understand before being understood?

Do your research. Michael, in the last chapter, had reasons to reconsider his approach when moving from South Africa to the U.S. after getting lots of rejections and radio silence in his applications. He knew he would be competing with local technology leaders and he was looking for any advantage he could gain to get his foot in the door.

He started by researching the technology employers in the areas he was interested in, which was Austin. Who was hiring? Why were they hiring? He used our approach from the last chapter. Google first, then LinkedIn, then Employer websites, and finally Glassdoor as the primary points. * Pro Tip - He also added Wired.com and Techcrunch.com to keep ahead of technology trends and hiring announcements. By highlighting his specific product, sector experience and change leadership examples, he was able to get valuable face to face time. Knowing that some of these companies were in change mode whether growth or recession or other forms of change, he knew that these types of employers always need good leadership to steer the ship. He highlighted that in his email/ calls /resume, and this was attractive to potential employers. We will go into this in more detail in the next chapter.

Taking your time to build an understanding of your value-based network (hiring managers) will help set yourself up for success.

Create an Achievement-Based Resume

According to Time magazine, the average hiring manager will spend less than six seconds reading your resume[vi]. Therefore, that document is a key tool in the art of communicating your achievements. I can attest to this in my role. Resumes that make direct impact with relevance and achievements have more chance of grabbing my attention and the attention of my employer clients.

It is all about your achievements and your ability to communicate them. You have to create an urgent need in the hiring manager's mind to meet you **(ask yourself, if you were the hiring manager, why would you take the time to meet you?).** Using your research above, build that pull from the hiring manager. Let us deconstruct the document to reassemble it in a way that will be most beneficial.

Grab Attention

You must grab attention or someone else will. And remember, you have six seconds or less.

- If you are going for a sales role, provide sales improvement results using clear numbers

- If you are going for a leadership role, identify headcounts, achievements, and results from your teams

- If your target role has P&L responsibilities, make sure to add the value of the P&L you were responsible for and how you grew the business

- If you are approaching a company in recession or pandemic give them examples of what you have achieved in times of change

Making sure your achievements are the focal point of your resume makes it easier for the reviewer to see how you can add value. This seems simple but I see thousands of resumes each year that don't.

An example of moving to a more achievement-based resume and the effect it can have, is Lucy. Lucy is a degree-qualified civil engineering person who commissions, designs, and builds multi-million-pound bridge projects in the U.K. As she had family in North America and spent some summers there while growing up, she set a goal of working on big engineering projects there. But it wasn't going to be so easy, Lucy had a working visa for Canada but had struggled to get interviews as she was based in Scotland and had limited Canadian experience.

Lucy applied to a few roles but heard nothing back. She read the book and did all the points discussed with Peter, Ben and Michael. Interestingly when we reviewed her resume, she found that her project achievements and results were hidden. **Her** work was impressive, and Lucy had won multiple construction quality awards which had led to her securing a permanent role at a large construction consultancy business. There were limited project details on her resume.

Job Description Resumes V Achievement Based Resumes.

There is a big difference between a job description resume and an achievement-based resume. Lucy's resume was the typical job description resume and you really want to avoid this type of resume. Job description resumes are usually 3-10 pages long listing the tasks and responsibilities that you have; these bullet points can range from 5-50 points. This is creating a challenge, and even the most diligent hiring manager, employer or recruiter will struggle to finish the document.

According to Glassdoor, an average corporate role will receive 250 applicants. Put yourself in the recruiter's shoes – would you prefer a tailored and customized achievement-based resume or a 6-page downloading of 'what I do?'

Lucy had realized that she had a job description resume and spent some time to go through each project and build it into the resume. She then adopted the *The Work Connection* resume formula of 2-3 lines in each role, list your role and responsibilities and any promotions. Then building out 3-5 bullet point of quantitative achievements, she had built a much more effective document at communicating her value.

Civil Engineering is very specialized and on her target lists there were a few employers that she had applied to before and not heard back from. Using the system that Peter, Ben and

Michael had applied and by effectively communicating her *value* through an achievement-based resume directly to a decision maker, Lucy was able to secure her target role in Vancouver with a large engineering consultancy business. There is no doubt her ability to bring her projects to life on her resume was a key factor in getting Lucy through the door. Now Lucy enjoys spending time with new friends and her family whilst building bridges all over North America.

Focus on Achievements and Results

You have a very small window to make an impression and you want that impression to be a positive one, remember that it's not really all about you, it's about understanding the hiring manager needs and matching that with your achievements based resume and communications.

Let's look at a proven resume structure that works – Marie's resume is a good starting point.

Marie Odin

123 E 78th St Apt 17D, New York, N.Y. 10343
Email: mcodin@cloud.com - Phone (212) 555 7777

PROFESSIONAL SUMMARY

Sr Vice President of Sales, Strong Marketing History
Account Management - B2C Sales - Channel sales - Business Development
Top performing salesperson in U.S.- Presidents Club in 2018 - Managed wholesale sales of $200 millionLifted market share from less that 2% to 17% in 5 years.

EXPERIENCE

Vice President of Sales, Metro Products   2014 - Present
NEW YORK, NEW YORK

Core Products equipment for all radiology - Pace Technologies: diagnostics radiology, ultrasound,nuclear medicine, special procedures, CT scan and MRI: cardiology related: patient monitor. EXG cardiac stress.

- Led a team of 142: 130 account manager, 12 regional managers.
- 125 Million in sales from 40 million start in 2014.
- Provided leadership key to the successful transition of company for regional to national market
- Personally interview, hired and trained approximately 100 account managers and 8 managers.
- Reported directly to Jupiter Medical owners and to Altran Medical National HQ

Senior Product Manager, Metro Products   2012 - 2014
NEW YORK, NEW YORK

- Achieved President Club in 2012,13 and 14. Top 5% region three consecutive years.
- Grew region from start up, to $55 million in 24 months
- Ranked 9 th out of 800 in achieving sales
- Expanded market share outside five boroughs to upstate New York to NJ and doubled revenue.

Product Manager, Parker Media   2010 - 2012
COLUMBUS, OHIO

- Top 5% region three consecutive years.
- Oversaw quality assurance as project lead
- Implimented new quality control standards

EXPERIENCE

Vice President of Sales, Metro Products   2014 - Present
NEW YORK, NEW YORK

Core Products equipment for all radiology - Pace Technologies: diagnostics radiology, ultrasound,nuclear medicine, special procedures, CT scan and MRI: cardiology related: patient monitor, EXG cardiac stress.

- Led a team of 142: 130 account manager, 12 regional managers.
- 125 Million in sales from 40 million start in 2014.
- Provided leadership key to the successful transition of company for regional to national market
- Personally interview, hired and trained approximately 100 account managers and 8 managers.
- Reported directly to Jupiter Medical owners and to Altran Medical National HQ

ProTips from Marie's resume format.

1. Keep the resume as close to **two pages** as you can.

2. **Start with your name, address, and contact details**. If you are looking for work and are serious about it, be sure to include your contact details including your mobile/cell number.

3. Professional summary section. **Be specific on achievements and use numbers early,** especially, if you are looking to approach a business in your sector. (Marie focused on High performing B2B sales early at the VP level, for example.)

4. In your employment history, - Take two or three lines *maximum* to explain **what it is you do,** and then use your achievements and results from the Achievements and Results exercise. (Marie does a great job below.)

The Work Connection

Senior Product Manager, Metro Products 2012 – 2014
NEW YORK, NEW YORK

- Achieved President Club in 2012,13 and 14. Top 5% region three consecutive years.
- Grew region from start up, to $55 million in 24 months
- Ranked 9 th out of 800 in achieving sales
- Expanded market share outside five boroughs to upstate New York to NJ and doubled revenue.

Be clear in your education and certification section. Only list what you feel will be relevant to your hiring manager.

Challenge #4: How does your resume look?

Be honest, is your resume more of a job description or achievement focused resume? If you had to mark it out of ten from a hiring managers perspective, how would you score it? If it's a 6/10, how can we get it to an 8 or 9/10?

For Lucy, that was as simple as doing the following: Use Marie's resume format, under each job take 2-3 lines, list your role, size of team responsibilities and any promotions. Then build out 3-5 bullet point quantitative achievements. This will allow you to build a more effective document at communicating your value. Include examples of achievement and results where you have worked directly with a hiring manager or as part of a team to achieve a goal. **In times of recession cost reductions or procedural improvements are also highly valuable.**

Then Pick 3.

Start by looking at the projects or solutions you have led or in which you played a significant part. Work through your resume, going through each role. Pick your best three **quantitative** examples of achievements and results you have delivered in line with your target employer and destination statement. The three that best demonstrate your ability to achieve and the skills you feel the target employer would need. **Numbers are key**. Be specific. Save these as you will be using them later in the interview process.

To save you time and develop a quality resume, go to theworkconnectionacademy.com/bullet register and we will send you Marie's full template to save you time and money.

The Approach

Now that we understand the target group, developed communications and an achievement-based resume to get your foot in the door, it is time to approach your Value-Based Network directly.

Creating a strong LinkedIn profile is an important step, too. If you are the product, your LinkedIn profile and resume are your "virtual shop window." It is only as good as the information that you add to it. Each available section should be filled out, from education to experience to board positions, community groups, and volunteering.

Ask yourself, "If you were the hiring manager for that role, what would you be looking for if you were reviewing your LinkedIn profile?"

Be sure to list your achievements and projects where appropriate and take the time to fill it out completely. Include a profile picture. Making sure your LinkedIn profile is as professional as it can be is a controllable step in approaching your Value-Based Network. Make sure it communicates a strong first impression.

LinkedIn has a group function, and you can connect with industry groups and join conversations online. An option to consider is setting up a Twitter account to communicate on industry topics/professional hashtags is also a good way of getting your name out and having conversations with people in your industry.

Then move onto your old and current work colleagues, followed by school and college connections as appropriate. Create a personal message rather than a standard one. Remember to keep the message simple and personal to elevate your connection requests and start to build and nurture your network day by day, brick by brick.

Part of our process involves connecting over LinkedIn, and over the years I have been often been asked why reaching out through LinkedIn can be more effective than sending an introduction email.

1. **The Strength of Research and Relevance:** On LinkedIn you can review a person's profile, sector experience, education, and companies they have worked at quickly. That is not possible over an introduction email.

2. **Power of commonality**: When you receive an email from someone you don't know, you may have little idea who the person is or who they connected to. Alternatively, when you get a LinkedIn message, you quickly see their network, sector experience and any shared relationships with them and that you can reach out to and assess if you need to.

3. **There is an optical element to LinkedIn:** In LinkedIn you can see their profile, quickly glance at their bio and profile, and you can also access any videos they have posted.

This is all much more visceral than an email from someone you do not know.

In the end if you connect on a commonality, are credible, relevant, and polite both email and LinkedIn can be effective.

Here is an email template that has been refined and used by hundreds of theworkconnectionacademy.com readers to connect with hiring managers. Please feel free to copy and edit for your own use. It has a marketing focus so be sure to update it for your area of expertise.

Subject line: Connecting

Hi _____,

My name is Sarah. I really love your company's work on the _____ brand launch. My family and I have just moved to your area. I have launched similar brands successfully (insert relevant brand achievements) in your sector.

The reason for contacting you is I would love to connect with you and learn more about your vision for your team and the brand as I am interviewing for (insert target role) in similar businesses.

Would the week of the 23rd or 30th work for a 15-minute conversation and a coffee/zoom/teams call?

Regards, Sarah.

This kind of approach works because:

It leads with a warm and credible introduction followed up by a statement that shows you can add value to the contact - I have launched similar brands successfully (insert relevant brand achievements) in your sector based on specific sector experience.

It provides a real reason for communication.

There is a call-to-action (the meeting) and a thank you.

A call-to-action is a technique used in sales and marketing to prompt someone to give an immediate response, either a sale, a signup, a call, or an exchange of information. Suggesting meeting up as you are interviewing locally for a coffee with "Would the week of 23rd and 30th work for 15 minutes and a Zoom or coffee?" is more likely to elicit a response than a vague approach with no details.

When driving your approach toward your goal of a meeting or call with a hiring manager the next step will be a follow-up phone call. The process is LinkedIn message, then email, followed by a phone call is the cycle.

You should use the same approach on the phone. The hiring manager is probably busy, so be empathetic, respectful, and state the reason for your approach with a call to action. Below is a script that has worked for other people, please feel free to use it. A typical call should flow like this:

"Hi, it's _____. I am conscious of calling you in the middle of your workday. Is it ok to speak? Y/N Thank you for your time. I appreciate it. I love what you are doing with x brand, the work is great. I have launched similar brands like x and y and x and y company myself. I have just moved to the area at _____. I have been following your work in _____ & _____ on the website - How did the launch go? We found when we launched this happened _____. How are the plans looking for next year? I would love to learn more about the team. I am interviewing at a couple of local businesses and would love to connect with you (in person -

Pandemic permitting) for a coffee or a Microsoft Teams/Zoom call. Would the week commencing 23/30th work to connect?

- Be humble and appreciative by thanking them for their time
- Introduce who you are and the reason for your call
- Ask them if now a good time is to chat

People often have a fear of "cold calling" or emailing hiring managers directly. However, this is not a "cold call", **part of most hiring managers' role is connecting with good people. If that's not something they typically do as part of their job, whether in good times or bad, they might not be a hiring manager, you want to connect with in the first place.** I know from my own experience that if you are polite, credible, and offer some relevant value to the person on the call (like a relevant achievement-based project or product you have worked on that you know through your research they are developing), that would fit in his or her team, you increase your chance of the time you want.

Your network build and numbers to be aware of.

We have helped hundreds of people to land the job they want through the C.A.L.M. **(Clarity. Attract. Land. Maintain.)** system and learn a few things along the way we want to share. **Please hear this - expect no or silence to start with, being patient and persistent in action will reward you at the end.** Deferred gratification in anything is hard and if you ever tried to lose weight without eating better and exercising the same goes. It is the same with this process. It is in a disciplined process, add your contact and contact them every week and keep building your network. You will be rewarded in the end. So, when those voices appear in your head "Why am I doing this? I'll just go back to job ads and take my chances" That's quite normal, don't sweat it but recognize them for what they are – FEAR of the unknown and get back to work and your network build. That is where the control lies in your action.

The Law of 7. In general marketing terms, it is said that it takes 7 interactions with someone before they will buy your product or service. Yet people get disheartened by their first direct no or no response from a potential employer. This is a targeted seed setting process. **So, don't expect a yes, the first time, stretch your timeline and improve your consistency of communication.** Keep to your system of communicating around connection, value you can add, and building understanding of them. Add your details to Marie's template at theworkconnectionacademy.com/bullet and don't be tempted to take short cuts like 'Hi, I'm David are you hiring?' That is a direct way to get a no or to get no response.

In email marketing terms, a response rate of 1-2% is acceptable for many industry norms. Our C.A.L.M. System encourages an opening group of 2 or 3 sectors of 35 employers with 1 contact in each. For 2 sectors that is circa 70 employers with 70 potential connections. Our response rate averages at 8%. **Our advice is to have at least over 70 real target connection with accurate email addresses**

and work on the quality of your win/win

communications to that group. That means if you have created the base of 70 contacts. Responses of yes and no begin to come back at 8%. For example, if you have 20 contacts and have the system average of 8% response that is 1.6 responses per communication. That is too small of a group and setting yourself up for failure. **In summary, build your base (contact group to a minimum of 70 real contacts) and you are setting yourself up for success in the first two weeks. 7 contacts x 10 days.**

If you look at the timelines for Peter and Ben, it gives you a real-life benchmark:

Step 1. Post Destination Statement, they used week 1 and 2 to research and build their contacts list of names of contact details. Ben used two sectors adding one per employer in two sectors circa 70 employers = 70 contacts. 7 Contacts x 10 days added to his lists.

Step 2. Week 2-4, the approach began with LinkedIn messages, followed by email and a phone call to 70 people (the hiring manager group). They divided them into x 7 groups of 10 people. Then when completed, cleaning data, and seeing who has responded etc., what emails were incorrect?"

Step 3. Week 4-6 the first yes responses start to appear. Continuing the 70 communications activity every week. Interviews and calls begin.

Step 4. Weeks 6-12, interviews, update the data and maintain.

Both Ben and Peter had their offers closed in this timescale.

Step 5. Weeks 12-48.

The process continues if you are looking for the right offer. These are three benchmarks that other professionals have found useful. **Which group best describes your situation?**

- **Group 1 – You are going through a career change or job hunt and are needing a new role.** Connect with five hiring managers per month. That is sixty new connections per year.

- **Group 2 – You don't like your job and want a better one.** Build a connection with three new hiring managers per month as above. In one year, that's thirty-six connections by year end.

- **Group 3 - You are in work and happy but want to build your network as a backup.** Connect with one new hiring manager per month out of your network. By year's end you will have twelve new value-adding connections.

Focus on the process and upping the quality of your data and approach rather than the no responses.

In follow up terms once a week is acceptable by phone or email. If you don't hear back in month one, give them a few weeks off and then re-approach and repeat the cycle. If you don't make a connection in month two or three, it is worth looking at getting a different hiring manager or connection into the employer.

You have a better chance of getting some face to face time if you package the approach as a win/win scenario. This was the case of a reader of ours at theworkconnectionacademy.com, Sarah.

Before taking some time off work to raise her family, she had been a successful marketing director in a consumer-packaged goods business. She was based in Boston, U.S. Like most returning parents, she was mindful of the day she would return to work and did her best to keep up with industrial innovations, technology, trade publications and select parts of her network. Three years out of the workforce, she began applying for work in her target area.

Sarah had read the book eleven months after she began her job search and the applications were not netting any return, in her view, they matched her marketing and consumer packaged goods expertise.

So why was she not getting interviews?

In summary, here is what we found.

- Playing in 30% online job ads space limited her options
- Not having a network of employers in her new area did not help
- She had an average resume

Good news - these were all things she could fix! Here are a few relevant things that we learned from our time with Sarah:

- Sarah is a great communicator; she is confident and professional face-to-face. We knew that if she could get her foot in the door and in front of destination employers, she would be able to demonstrate how she could make a great addition
- Financially, her family needed the extra income

ASAP

- Being out of the loop for a while, Sarah had done the typical Job Search 1.0. Applying for the job postings she should be and approached her old network, and they had delivered very little. It was time to go a different Job Search 2.0 route and build a new network by going directly to the employers

- Sarah and her family were now in the suburbs approximately 1 hour and 20 minutes away from the downtown area

- The resume she had prepared was a solid 6 out of 10. Not earth-shattering but could be improved with some Achievement and Results work

These are the actions she decided to do:

- Like the Ben, Peter, and Michael she went through the same system Career Compass, Destination Statement, List Building, and Value Based Network (Research) approach. That didn't take long she knew what she wanted and why?

- She went through Challenge #4 taking her resume to be more achievement-based. Focusing on the hiring managers' needs she had found through the research stage

- Having moved out of the city, where some of the bigger employers were. She began building out a target list of employers who she would love to work for locally

- She used our email template and call template to begin to build her own network

Within two months, the interviews started happening. Within three months, she had two job offers. She opted to work for one run by two women founders and is now enjoying plotting the route to growth using her own set of unique marketing skills. Interestingly, when I chatted with the founders, they were so happy that Sarah made the effort to connect with them directly. They had an open marketing role for four months and found no one of her caliber.

Remember, there are always good employers looking for good people and think win-win!

Takeaways:

- **Key Principle: Proactivity, Research, and Courage**

- Build understanding before being understood. Through research, build an understanding of your destination employers, their teams, and their hiring managers *before* approaching them. Creating a "pull" from your group

- Elevate yourself as a candidate with an achievement and result based resume. You have a small window to make an impression. Make the most of it

- Connect on a commonality, have a compelling reason for approaching someone. Have a clear call to-action, be consistent in your follow up. If you do not, don't expect a response

- **The Law of 7.** Expect responses of no and silence – your focus should be on the process, don't sell first. Expect to ask 7 times before a yes or no

- **Be professional always and be relevant.** If this is your chosen sector? Where you are going to be spending a third of your life in it, enjoy meeting people and show a genuine interest. This never fails to impress people

- **Post COVID-19, remember to be kind, everyone has their own struggles**

Chapter 5: Land It. Part 1

Turning Interviews into Offers

The battle for competitive roles is often won before the interview has even taken place. You have done your research, created your lists and contacted those hiring managers who are truly the decision-makers. This has led to achieving your first goal, contact time with a targeted hiring manager. It is now time to ensure that your preparation leads you down the path towards success, not just in the relationship, but also interview, and if the opportunity presents itself to a job offer. Improving your interview skills is critical in beating the competition.

We have distilled down what we have learned over 15 years, into a 3-stage process: Pre, during and post-interview. This chapter covers the pre interview stage.

In being part of well over 10,000 interviews in my career, **it is often not the best candidate that gets the job offer. It is the candidate that is best prepared and who performs best during the interview process.** The good news is that this is a battle that you can control and win if you want to.

Pre-Interview

Once you have secured an appointment for a meeting/ interview with your hiring manager, follow the next steps in preparation for it.

Step 1: What are your goals in this hiring process?

You would be surprised at the number of people who go into their interviews without a plan or any goals. They are so happy to have any connection with an employer that they focus on some research and examples and trust their personality to pull them through.

The truth is that you have worked hard to get in front of the interviewer, but it can be worth little if you don't know what success would look like for you? To use an athlete analogy, you wouldn't train all year only to not turn up and perform on game day. Here are some questions to help you prepare for an interview by setting some success criteria:

• What are the goal(s) you would like to achieve from the interview/meeting? For example, maybe you want to find out more about the employer, the hiring manager, their team, and opportunities for growth or how secure the employer is? Or it could be as simple as getting a second interview

• How are you going to achieve those goals? Be specific. What resources will you need to achieve these goals? Research/ time/ practice?

• **What are the three critical things you need to understand to feel comfortable in accepting an offer at this**

business? This is personal for every individual and is based on your Destination Statement. For Ben back in Chapter 2, it was understanding their policy on work flexibility, compensation, and security of the business as he had just been laid off. For you, it could be a better role, a better boss, or just something as simple as a secure job close to home, paying a salary you need

If you are comfortable that you know what success looks like (by setting your goals), you have a better chance of achieving it and reviewing your progress as you go through an interview process. For your next interview, set out clear goals of what you would like to achieve and work towards them.

Step 2: Your Pre-Interview Review

Your pre interview process is a tick list that our theworkconnectionacademy.com readers use to demonstrate how to research the business first, then the team, and then the role. It has the effect of allowing you to see more of the potential opportunity. In the case of many desirable employers, whether you go directly or are directed via a pre-existing job, you are entering a competitive process and your aim during the interview stage is to be the last person standing.

The goal of this next section is to equip you with a sound base of research surrounding each part of the opportunity and to identify that point of difference that will make you stand out. It has the added benefit of allowing you to assess the entire role, not just the day to day tasks you will be doing.

To achieve your interview goals and assess if this is the right role for you, you will need to increase your knowledge of these three areas below.

Find out why this employer is hiring? As discussed previously, you have already created a picture using tools like Google, LinkedIn, Glassdoor, and the employer's website to research the company. Reasons for hiring can include someone leaving the business, growth of the business or an immediate need driven by an event like a new business win. For example - If you have used Google to search the company name and hiring or the year you will get articles on publicized events.

Team and hiring manager. Use Google, LinkedIn, and Glassdoor to research the people involved and their teams. What are their technical and educational backgrounds? Are there any patterns in their team members? Length of service, education, or relevant experience? Are there any gaps in the team? Building knowledge of names and teams can show your conscientiousness. This deeper research of the team and your potential boss is an important step in building understanding of whether you want to join the group. Rather than figuring out that after the fact, that the job is not for you. You are interviewing them as much as they are interviewing you.

The Role. Using the C.A.L.M system, you have already defined the role(s) you are going for. That role will have a technical part, defined by the technical prerequisites of the role, and the individual requirements including soft skills, people, leadership, organization, and cultural needs.

Be sure to do your research. What background do other people doing your target job have? Skills, experience, common traits? If you are better than what you see, great. If not, how will you improve?

Your Point of Difference

In the ever-increasing competitive landscape of employment, differentiation from your competition can make all the difference. In sports, your point of difference is a term used widely in the hiring or the drafting process. These points can add considerable value to the wider team. In business an example would be, if you are a salesperson and are applying to a sales leadership role in a beverage company, you may have worked on a big account in that specific category. Being able to communicate this effectively is a keyway to elevating your application and showing the hiring manager you are dialed into their needs. **Lean into this** and know it well pre interview. In competitive job markets that we mentioned at the start of the book, these **incremental improvements** can often be the difference between you landing the role you want or not.

Challenge 5: Point of Difference

In the next ten minutes, think of what your point of difference is for your target role. For example, finish the sentence "I have. . ."

- Built a team in a recession
- Managed through adversity

- Worked on a piece of software used by the company I want to work for
- Developed a product the company is now making
- Manufactured a process the company has a version of
- Sold a competitive brand and been successful

In your pre interview review when preparing for an interview, it is good to look at the challenge not from your own viewpoint but from that of the hiring manager.

The hiring manager is a human being like everyone else, just because they sit on the other side of the table does not make them a superhero. Hiring someone can be a challenging process. The cost of getting a hire wrong can run into tens or even hundreds of thousands of dollars/pounds/euro. The very fact that they are interested in meeting is an indication that they may need the right additional resources to get more done. Like everyone else during an economic downturn, employers, hiring managers, and recruiters are feeling extra stress, so turn that empathy up. To set yourself up for success, prepare accordingly.

There are two objectives of the **Pre-Interview Review**: Research to find what the hiring manager wants and give it to them. Then research to find what you want to know to feel secure in accepting an offer with this employer. Knowing these points can not only raise your interview performance but also save you years of time in accepting the wrong role.

Challenge 6: Building understanding of what the hiring manager is looking for?

Using your research from your pre-interview review and from your Destination Statement add your top three key things a hiring manager would be looking for in that role. As a guide you can use both technical and individual needs as well as your point of difference for this role.

If you are stuck, go to linked job search and type in your job title. It will take you to job advertisements and either in the responsibilities or summary sections they will talk about what they need this person to achieve.

- Technical
- Personal
- Cultural / Point of Difference

We have found that people who take their time to research then review these needs have a much better return from the interview process. Take your time and use the research to build an accurate picture of what the employer is looking for before going in. **You will see how it allows you to be more focused, be yourself, be prepared, and perform better.**

The STAR Method.

Your ability to communicate your value, achievements and experience will be a key skill set in the interview process. Post Covid-19 you have a small window to make an impression face to face or over video.

This method gives you a sense of control pre-interview because you will have three or four examples prepared so you can answer definitively and concisely. It will also give you an advantage over your competitive candidates as many do not apply this level of structure to their examples pre or during an interview.

The STAR method stands for Situation, Task, Action, Result.

Situation: a challenge, project, or event that you or your team or your business faced.

Task: what were you or your team's plans and responsibilities for the situation?

Action: what specific steps were taken to rectify the situation?

Result: what were the results of actions taken?

What is the STAR method and why is it important?

Behavioral interview questions usually revolve around a specific example or situation. They give the hiring manager a glimpse into your work ethic, how you think, your approach to challenges and your ability to work in a team. Some examples of behavioral interview questions include:

• Provide an example of when you went above and beyond for the customer or your team

• Tell me a specific thing about your favorite leader that made a positive impact on you

• Tell me about a time you had to make a difficult decision

- Tell me about a time when a co-worker was frustrated with you and how you handled it
- Describe a time when you had to resolve conflict in the workplace
- Describe a situation in which you had to convince someone to complete a task your way or to do something they did not want to do
- Tell me about a time you set a goal and achieved it.
- Let's look at a real-life example and how a candidate answered this behavioral question: "Tell me about a time when you were under pressure and how you performed" The interview was for a Senior Vice President role, responsible for Regional General

Managers across the United States and the United Kingdom

There are three key outcomes for a Senior Vice President's role: **Sales and Marketing** - Can they sell and lead a sales team to grow in challenging times? **Finance and Operations** - Do they have experience with profit and loss ownership? **Team building and leadership** - Can they demonstrate the ability to hire and retain great talent? An impactful STAR example in line with these needs would include:

Situation. During the last recession in 2009, I had inherited a sales team of four people and $3 million in sales and grew it to 14 people and $21 million in three years. This exceeded our targets by 30%. With that level of growth, as we built the team out, the pressure to meet customer demand was strong and our on-time delivery drifted from two days to seven days.

Task. We had staked our name and reputation to these new customers on delivery, beating lead times. I pulled together a team from sales, logistics, and HQ and we did some analysis of our process and the delivery issues we were having.

Action. To address the problems, the team had daily calls and within a week, the key issues were isolated, and a process was put in place to address them.

Result. We reduced on-time delivery from seven days to one and a half days (our competitor's delivery was at four days). This allows us to keep our new customers and continue to grow.

What does that answer show the interviewer?

This shows the hiring manager clear organizational leadership, outcome-based skills and value achieved through times of change (a recession). The person is proactive and can work collaboratively. They have delivered sales. They are self-aware enough to spot the problem and get it solved. They are customer-focused and conscientious.

Challenge 7: Your First STAR

From Challenge 6 take the three key outcomes that a hiring manager will be looking for in your target role, pick one and prepare your first STAR example. Keep in mind the notion of problem, solution, result.

Why this Business, Team, and Role?

This is a scenario that we see play out over and over, when a candidate does a tremendous job in preparing and answering questions and asking powerful questions of their own, then they close down and forget to tell the hiring manager--why they want the role? **In a competitive process, the candidate who can get across their whys is often at an advantage as they have truly connected with the interviewer.**

Key things to mention when talking about your whys:

Make the match. If interviewing in a family-run employer, use "I have a history of delivery in family businesses." Be specific with your Why's. In a sales team role, you may include your; enjoyment of working in a result orientated culture, hitting, and exceeding targets, and working with teams. "Having taken some time to research the culture in your business, and meet with you and the team, this is definitely a company I could see myself adding value to."

Be relevant. "Having launched product lines similar to those we have discussed, I would love the opportunity to learn your way and hit the ground running for you and the team." "With your new product line and continued growth, I am really attracted to adding value to your team."

Try to avoid why's that may turn off the hiring manager. "Your location is near my home." Or "I am looking to earn more money." Or "I am out of work and looking." These demonstrate a real lack of emotional intelligence and conscientiousness.

Lower stress to perform.

The answers to the following questions will not only serve to calm your mind pre-interview but also to set you up for success during the interview. These can be asked over a phone /zoom call or email pre interview.

• Who will I be meeting? Be sure that you understand their names and job titles

• What will be the format of the meeting/ interview?

• How long will it last? I have had candidates who have turned up for interviews before and been there for three or four hours, so make sure you are fueled appropriately

• Is there anything I should bring? Always have additional up-to-date copies of your resume with you. Some roles like marketing creatives or software designers require a web page or portfolio. Ask before meeting if this would be helpful. In some cases, it can be the difference between closing and not closing

Takeaways:

• **Key Principle: Being prepared leads to performance**

• **Pre-interview preparation will help you to separate yourself from the pack**. There are many things in the hiring process you can't control - This is within your control

• **Champions do extras** - In a process where it often comes down to you and another candidate, **it is often these incremental 1% preparation points that get you the offer**

• **Be sure to ask yourself, "If I was the hiring manager what would they want in a team member?"** See the interview process from the perspective of the hiring manager. This will really help lift the level of performance

- **Identify your Point of Difference and have your STAR examples** prepared pre interview to anticipate interview questions

- **Understand your whys - Why this employer, team, and role?** And be able to communicate the whys with them. These are often critical in getting close competitive offers over the line and landed

Chapter 6: Land It. Part 2

Turning Interviews into Offers

During the interview.

"Control the controllables" is a stoic philosophy that runs through the core of this book. It is important to try to control, as much as possible, what happens on the day of an interview so that you can concentrate on your interview performance such as your appearance, attitude, and your preparedness. Taking care of basics will free you up to do your best in front of the hiring manager.

Here are the 7 laws that will help you ace any interview, whether face to face, over phone or via video technology. Go through them methodically so it makes you feel confident rather than overwhelmed. By completing it, you are preparing yourself to be confident and ready to perform in the interview.

Law 1. The Basics

- Be appropriately dressed and groomed. Dress smart, feel smart, act smart
- Be on time
- Make eye contact with the interviewer
- Speak up
- Do not interrupt
- Be polite

- For phone or video interviews, make sure your technology is ready for use by pretesting

Law 2. Body Language and its importance on how you are perceived.

Adding to the basics above, close your eyes and picture the following scenario. You have targeted the company you want to work with and secured an interview with the hiring manager. In the interview, you have prepared excellently, you nail your STAR examples, and your questions create a flow in the interview. All the while you are slouching in your seat, fidgeting, and looking at the floor. All your work is for nothing if your posture is poor and your body language is not dialed in.

In virtual interviews and face to face, our posture and body language is so important. Your body is designed to give off extremely powerful and meaningful signals. Our nonverbal communication is over 50% of how communication is understood by the other person. Power poses pre-interview work. In your car, cubicle, or train, take a few moments and practice, open your arms wide with your shoulder blades pulled together. Inhaling for 6 seconds and exhaling for 6 seconds, 10 times allows you to control how you feel. What is the body language like of someone you consider to be powerful? How do they carry themselves? Mirror that.

Law 3. Your relevant examples

If you are asked a question, answer it, don't answer what you think you hear. Answer all questions with pertinent relevant examples. Using the STAR technique in your preparation will give you an advantage. Sharpen those pre-interview answers. If your target role has a leadership element, give genuine STAR examples that show your performance with leading people and teams.

Conscientiousness is the number one pre-requisite when it comes to job performance. Make sure your STAR examples demonstrate your conscientiousness and your ability to deliver results.

If you are in any doubt as to what is meant by the question over Zoom or in the room, just ask them to repeat the question please. That will buy you a few extra seconds to truly listen.

Law 4. Conversation and Flow

According to a recent MIT study, successful candidates follow the 50/50 rule. In other words, they listened almost as much as they talked in an interview scenario. Successful candidates tend to let the employer do the talking for approximately one half of the interview. This appears natural and helps build credibility. Remember, every meeting is unique, and your credibility is built through your energy, work-based or STAR examples and how the employer can envision you fitting with the team.

In our experience, most people like talking about themselves. In the questions section of the interview, we recommended asking the interviewer "why did you join the business" questions. According to a study in *Psychology Today*, "talking about oneself activates the same areas of the brain that light up when eating good food, taking drugs, and even having sex. Simply put, self-disclosure is gratifying. It gives us a neurological buzz."[vii]

Power Question Tips to create flow in an interview:

- If I were successful in getting the role and we were in our 12-month review - What is the number 1 priority you would like completed in Year 1?
- What separates the top performers from the average in your business?
- How would you describe the ideal candidate?
- What are the top 2 traits that you are looking for?

Pro Tip, during times of change like recession or pandemic, do not underestimate how important it is to get across your ability to perform in these challenging times If the business is going through change or is in need of leadership and management is part of the role, ask questions about the team's strengths and challenges. **An example would be – Post Covid-19, if you were to improve one thing from the team's performance, what would it be?** Listen to them and then give a relevant STAR example. In self-awareness terms, you can't profess to be a great leader if you demonstrate no interest or care for the people and their operational effectiveness

Law 5. Previous Employers. Never say anything negative about previous employers. If, for whatever reason, you have had a negative experience leaving a business, use the following conversation technique.

"Through that period, lots of change had happened. I helped hit the targets in my department by delivering x and y and achieved a lot of what we had set out to with the CEO. In leaving, I still have a strong relationship with the CEO."

Law 6. Closing the Interview

As the interview begins to wind down, this is a great opportunity for you to ask any additional questions you may have. You should confirm their contact details, obtain a business card, and ask for clarity about the next steps and what you should expect. For example, "If I am successful in this round of interviews, when would the next round of interviews be and with whom?" You may also want to boldly ask, **"Knowing what you know about the role, is there anything that would stop you from hiring me?**

Before closing the interview, ask yourself – "Do I know the process by which a decision is made, and what is the timeline?"

After the interview

Law 7. Follow Up

Finish Strong. You should always follow up, send a thankyou note or a follow-up email. This is a great way to underline your stated points and thank them genuinely for their time. Whether you are writing a handwritten note or an email, keep it short and to the point.

If you consider *The Work Connection* philosophy this is about building a network for you to help others and for others to help you. **Every interview, successful or not, is a human touch**

point to build another connection for that network. Think of Michael and the analyst; both left interviews not being hired, but in connecting with a potential employer with a giver mentality, that led to the two of them being hired.

You never know when you might meet this person again so, either way, you want to leave a good impression. As we have seen, although this hiring manager may not see you as a fit for this job, they may refer you to another department or company. This happens more than you think.

In the 24 hours after the interview, it is good practice to take ten minutes to reflect on the interview. Evaluate your preparation. Could the preparation have been better? Review the Interview. What could have been improved? How would you rate your performance? It is important in your review of the interview to focus on what went well. Think about emphasizing or evolving those practices in the next interview. That way you will continue to sharpen your skills and stay ahead of the competition.

Takeaways:

- **Key Principle: Control the controllables.** You can control your timing, technology, attitude, preparedness, body language, and how you are dressed

- **Create a conversational flow** by asking relevant questions and listening to their answers

- **You are interviewing them as much as they are interviewing you.** To do that you need to establish what your goals are?

- **Preparation is the key** to answering questions about yourself
- **Know your whys**. Why are you interviewing with the employer and communicating this to them.
- **Connect with the interviewer** and get across your reason why you would perform in the role
- **Make sure to finish strong,** follow up and reinforce key points succinctly

Chapter 7: Land It. Part 3

Assess, Accept, or Reject

Congratulations, the employer has presented you with a written job offer. Take a moment to reflect and say, "Well done!"

Now, what do you do?

Having processed thousands of job offers over the years, we know that there are some common behaviors that successful candidates use again and again when assessing, negotiating, accepting, or rejecting job offers. **The goal of this chapter is to share our advice so you can guide yourself through the process successfully and ensure you arrive in your role happy with your job offer and looking forward and ready to perform.**

Post Covid-19 we understand that in times of less jobs, more competition or career change, you may want to take the first offer that comes in. That is your choice. This chapter is a simple guide to assess the offer you receive, in the end in each individual situation you will know best.

From the beginning of this process, we have talked about value and specifically, the value you can deliver to the employer. We will also make you aware of some of the numbers in the wider job market when it comes to offer management. Through this exposure to the assessment and market, you can build a sense of your value and develop a plan to close an offer that matches that value.

Be aware that neither a verbal nor a written offer is legally binding unless it has the employment contract included. An employment contract is only legally binding if signed by both parties. If you are in any doubt of your job offer, make sure to check with a local employment lawyer. As information in this book is not meant as legal advice. In terms of a full job offer, what we mean here is a written job offer letter with a supporting contract of employment. **Again, if in doubt speak to a local employment lawyer**

The Start Point.

There is usually goodwill and attraction at the point of a job offer and you have the leverage to use it or not, as you choose. Given that this new company likes you enough to make you an offer and you like them enough to spend some time getting to know them, this is as good a time as any to ask questions and be reflective of your whys and to see if this employer matches up to them.

At this stage, having a wider lens on your bigger goals (your Destination Statement) will be helpful as the tendency is to launch into micro-detail like bonuses, pension plans and healthcare insurance first. It is common to feel rushed at this point for several reasons. You may experience a mix of emotions from being excited to relieved. Now more than ever with volatility growing keep your guard up. So just take a breath and remember when others rush, take your time and reflect. However excited you may be to have the job offer; it pays to ask some rudimentary questions before accepting an offer. Employers can rack up the pressure, too, by asking for answers as soon as possible. Remain calm and follow the process outlined below:

Assessment and Prioritization

One of the main objectives of an interview is to get an offer. The objective of the Offer Management stage is different, now, you need to review and prioritize the offer, then negotiate to see if you would like to accept it or reject it politely and move on. Remember, nothing is won yet. We have lost count of the number of times when people have "switched off" at the offer stage and the offer has been "pulled" from the client.

Now is the time to take your work life, lifestyle, family life, and destination priorities from Chapter Two and compare them to your offer. Where do they match up? Where do you want to negotiate so they are more aligned?

An offer is made up of different parts. Some people tend to focus on the salary number at this stage, but the salary should be just one part of your decision-making. Look at the offer number as a whole rather than getting hooked into concentrating on your base salary--you need to consider bonuses, commissions, pension contributions, and health insurance contributions depending on what country you live in. Also, remember to factor in the effect of income tax on your real or net number.

What is someone with my experience, work ethic, and skill level being paid in this location? Salary.com, Glassdoor and LinkedIn can support your review and give you a better idea if the offer is in line with industry standards.

Connect with head-hunters or recruiters in your sector and open up that you are looking at options. It is a win/win for both parties. We get access to you as a potential candidate and you get to ask questions. Ask us directly about salary benchmarks in your sector. Sometimes these can change dramatically from location to location and from job to job. It is important to know this type of information before you accept an offer rather than figuring it out a few months into your new role. Speaking as one myself, we can be an invaluable resource for information when looking at researching the salary and benefits that are offered in your industry, sector, and for your skillset.

Be aware, if you are in a demand job role in a high demand market, you may have more leverage when negotiating.

Speak with people you trust. They can be a sounding board to run ideas by as well as provide their input since they may be affected by your work decision. Trusted advisors and family members can give you the confidence you need to make the right decision. Think Michael, Sarah, Ben, Lucy, and Peter all consulted with their partners, family, or friends before accepting offers.

Important questions to consider include; If I do well and outperform, what does progression look like? Is there room for growth and development with the department and/or company?

Have there been any flags in any stage of assessing the employer's culture? They can include unprofessionalism in interviews, "low ball" offers where the salary and package are off industry norms, or sizable turnover of staff.

If the culture meets your needs, you can move on to evaluate it by asking the following questions:

- Are higher education, training, and development paid for?
- In countries where there is no supported national healthcare system - Who is covered by the healthcare benefits? Family or individual only?
- What is the vacation and sick time policy?
- Are you eligible for stock in the business?
- If relevant, what is the car allowance? Is there a fuel card?
- Are there supporting healthcare benefits? Gym etc.
- If a relocation is involved, is there an allowance or are your expenses reimbursed?
- What is the company policy on flexible working?
- What is the notice period and if any non-competes are included?
- What is cost and benefit breakdown of accepting this role versus starting the process again from scratch? This often makes you aware of other options available to you and helps in deciding

Alternatively, if the job offer gets you into an industry you want and has the majority of what you need you may be open to accepting the offer to get a foot in the door. This way, you can get an opportunity to learn, perform and progress.

Your Plan – If you don't ask you don't get.

Now that you have determined the parts of the offer that you would like to keep and the parts you would like to negotiate, it's time to put in a plan to negotiate, accept, or reject the offer. Candidates often underestimate the control they have in closing a job offer; this will help your confidence in getting what you want.

Who are you talking to?

You need to be aware of who you are dealing with. The C.A.L.M. system has been developed so you are dealing directly with a hiring manager. Whether the hiring manager, business owner or human resources person presents the offer, you must provide them with the appropriate questions and information in line with your assessment and priorities. If you come at it from the perspective of joint problem solving, there is a much greater chance of success.

Demonstrate Thoroughness

What are you flexible on? What questions would you like to ask? You cannot negotiate everything, and once you've agreed on something, it is challenging to go back on it.

The Way You Ask

In many situations in life it is not what you ask for, it is the way you ask for it that determines the outcome. It all comes back to that very important question that we have asked throughout this book: if you were in their position, how would you like to be asked the question? Your tone should be positive, and you should be organized around the points you would like to cover. Working together with the person presenting the offer to get it over the line.

Remember that it is completely normal to negotiate at this stage. Be strong and positive and this will set the tone for a business-like conversation.

Counteroffers

Negotiating your salary through a counteroffer is a solid first step and can often set a business relationship on a sound foundation if done in a professional, well-researched way. However, there are two things that you should be aware of when considering negotiating salary in your job offer:

If you have stated a salary earlier in the interview stage when asked, be careful that if you are asking for a higher number you have the research to justify it.

In salary negotiations, you should not be the first to say your desired salary and benefits. If you are placed in a situation where you must, then give a range. I have been earning x or y leading a team of x. The interviews I am in process with are in range from x-y.

If you have done the research and communicated your reasons for asking for more money respectfully and professionally, you can do no more. Refer to what and why of who you are, and what skills, achievements, and attributes you bring to the employer. When quoting research, talk in generalities such as "workforce database and companies of similar size and roles."

However, never directly quote the numbers on specific websites as these can be challenged for relevancy.

If the employer comes back to you with a second counteroffer, traditionally this is the bottom line. Don't be scared to ask for clarity on other points from this point on. Try to do it all at once before you ask and know your exit point. You want to make it as easy for the other person to give you what you are asking for, especially if they must speak to other decision-makers.

When everything is taken into consideration, they are offering you a job. Express gratitude, even if it's nothing close to what you're expecting. The objective here is to negotiate and agree to something that works for both sides. Be respectful and positive at all times. If your negotiations are successful, you will be working with these people. You will want to get things off on the right foot.

If an employer simply declines to move, you can accept and negotiate a review down the line on an agreed-upon timescale, or you can thank them and walk away. In fact, you can accept, negotiate, or walk away from the offer at any point. If through the negotiation process you keep getting "no" as an answer to your questions, it can be a sign of a company's unwillingness to compromise, and that can be an indication of their culture or management inflexibility. If this goes back to one of your reasons for looking, a lack of flexibility in your previous position, that might be enough for you to decline an offer.

Alternatively, if you have been out of work for some time and would love the role and can cope with things not being perfect, you may think, "I can work with this."

I work in an environment where hundreds of job offers are accepted, negotiated, and turned down every week. There is nothing wrong with deciding 'this is not for me.' There is nothing to be ashamed about turning down a job offer. In fact, if done in the right way, these relationships can be bridged in the future as suppliers, advisers, customers, or potential employers.

Here is an approach to turn down an offer.

Be genuine in your thanks.

"Thank you for the offer of the Operations Manager and the time in getting to know you, your team and the business. I wanted to express my appreciation for you and your team's time."

Get to the point about your reason.

"This position seems like a great opportunity. After careful reflection, I have decided to pursue another role. At this time, this role will offer me more opportunities to pursue my passion for x or y sector and work."

Protect the network.

"All the very best with your vision for the business. It's been a pleasure getting to know you, and I hope that we meet again in the future."

Takeaways:

- **Key Principle: take time to assess and prioritize your needs**
- Assess the offer by prioritizing each item in order of importance and alignment with your destination needs
- Pick out the items that you would like to negotiate
- Create a solid business case as to why your needs are important and present it to the hiring manager. Think "if I was the hiring manager, what is important for me?"
- The objective here is to negotiate and agree to something that works for both sides. Communicate with the same credibility and positivity that got you to this point
- Always consider your walkaway alternatives
- The goal is to walk into the role motivated, not looking over your shoulder thinking 'I should have asked for x or y'

Chapter 8: Maintain

What do you need to do to maintain and grow your relationships to give your career options?

Think back to Peter and what he said about, wishing he would have done a "little every year and quarter in building his connections". That way you will always have options. That is the approach we recommend.

Using the C.A.L.M (Clarity, Attract, Land and Maintain) system every year, we recommend the following as a guide to keep building and maintaining your connections.

• If you are going through a career change or job hunt, moving to a new country, connect with five people each month (hiring managers only). That is sixty new connections per year

• You are in work and happy; build a connection with one new person per month out of your network, someone in your sector who you would report to and whose work you admire. By year's end you will have twelve new value-adding connections

• You don't like your job and are considering options; build a connection with three new people per month as above. In one year, that's thirty-six connections by year end

AJOJ - Schedule it into your work calendar at the end of **A**pril, **J**uly, **O**ctober and **J**anuary. If you are part of our reader community at workconnectionacademy.com/bullet - We send out reminders to our group at these times to help you maintain and grow your network.

Little and Often - This continuity of effort will allow you to maintain what you have built and continue to prosper as a result. As with all things this goes up and down in life as you have the time. No pressure, no noise, just a quiet focus on your bigger goal of maintaining your options through your network. That way when you review at the end of the year you can see you are building equity in your network and have a back up plan.

We hope you get some value from the book and more importantly start using some of the tools in the book for yourself or recommend it to a friend who needs some new ideas and support in their career change or job hunt.

For our readers we have an offer to say thank you for taking your valuable time and reading the book.

YOUR FREE BOOK AND TEMPLATES USED IN THIS BOOK IS WAITING FOR YOU.

To say thank you for reading and share some extra value, we have a free giveaway.

Visit workconnectionacademy.com/bullet and we will give you the new templates of the resume used in this book and our latest book in *The Work Connection series* **-** ***From Zero to Interview*** *-* ***The proven three-step guide to getting the interviews you want, now.***

In today's post Covid-19 world this book is packed with real life case studies, resume and email templates to help you get interviews when you are being ghosted.

If you have any questions raised by the book, pop over to workconnectionacademy.com/bullet and we will respond ASAP.

Chapter 9: The Work Connection!

The premise at the start of the book is a manifesto to bring relationships back to your work life to help counter the effects of volatile economies, voluntary and involuntary events and technology on your work life.

This book will have been a success if you make one new connection or help one person in your new network. We hope you don't stop there.

It was written for those who are frustrated by the modern job search, and those willing to try a new approach. When used, the system helps:

- **The people who have lost their jobs because of the economy** and only see 30% of all the roles available

- **The people wanting more options & control in their work life.** Building a Value Based Professional Network, something that will be sustain you in good and bad economic times

- **The 98% of people** who don't get called to interview and end up settling for something they could get, rather than something they want

- **The people who spend a fortune of time and money on an education and haven't yet invested in their network to the same level**

- [vii]**The 87% people who are disengaged in their current role and know they could do better.** Gallup's State of the Global Workplace survey.

- **The people who were concerned about contacting employers directly**

Making important decisions based on the 30% of the available information is never good. Any step into the other 70% will be positive for the quality of your decision making and your career options.

There is also some comfort in knowing no matter how volatile the economy and the events get more troubling, you can build a network of your own that will give you more options.

The more volatility in the economy the more you need to invest in your relationships (network) and skills.

Better relationships = Better options = Better work life.

Thank you from all the workconnectionacademy.com team for taking the time to read the book. It really is appreciated.

Our goal with workconnectionacademy.com and the C.A.L.M. system is to help you get the best from your work life. It has helped hundreds of people like Peter, Sarah, Lucy, Ben, and Michael to take back control and elevate their work lives. It also helped the employers they now work for and who are grateful for finding these good people.

Remember, the world is full of good people looking for good people. Be proactive, get out there and connect with people and land the job you want.

The Work Connection

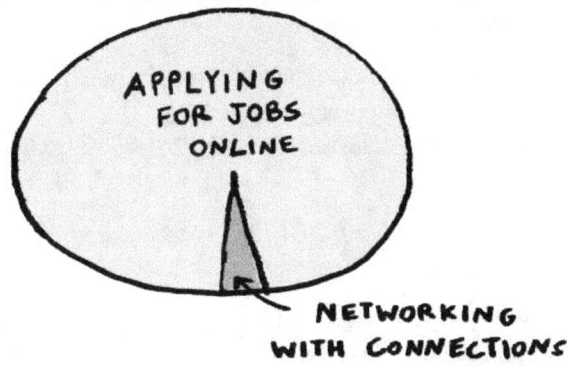

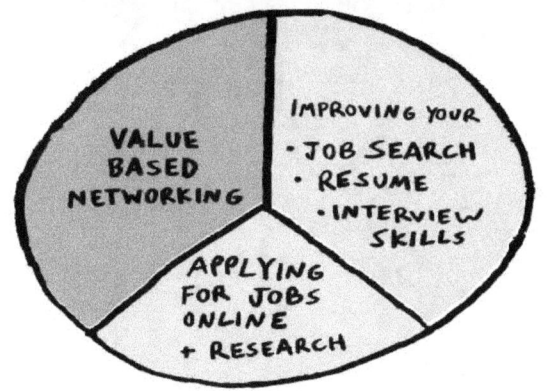

End Notes

[i] https://fortune.com/2016/05/10/baby-boomers-millennials-jobs/
[ii] https://www.forbes.com/sites/jeannemeister/2012/08/14/the-futureof-work-job-hopping-is-the-new-normal-formillennials/#f46e7e313b8e
[iii] https://www.statcan.gc.ca/eng/start

[iv] https://www.migrationpolicy.org/article/frequently-requestedstatistics-immigrants-and-immigration-united-states
[v] https://www.forbes.com/sites/stevedenning/2014/04/11/whysoftware-is-eating-the-world/

[vi] https://business.time.com/2012/04/13/how-to-make-your-resumelast-longer-than-6-seconds/

[vii] https://www.psychologytoday.com/ca/blog/positiveprescription/201703/why-we-love-talking-about-ourselves.

[viii] https://news.gallup.com/poll/165269/worldwide-employees-engaged-work.asp

www.ingramcontent.com/pod-product-compliance
Lightning Source LLC
Chambersburg PA
CBHW070656220526
45466CB00001B/466